Walking
with Christ

Walking with *Christ*

Life Stories of Jeanne Wieck Atkins

with Scriptural Reflections by
Stephanie Engelman

Cover Design by Stephanie Engelman
Layout by Stephanie Engelman

Printed in the United States of America
First Printing, 2020
ISBN 978-1-7345670-1-4

www.iwpersonalhistories.com
www.StephanieEngelman.com

Introduction
by Stephanie Engelman

When I met Jeanne Atkins less than a year ago, it was at the urging of several people within our north side Indianapolis Catholic community. "You've got to write Jeanne's story!" they insisted.

Looking back, I believe there were several reasons for their enthusiasm. First, Jeanne Atkins was (and is) a bit of an enigma, the impeccably dressed woman regularly seen at daily Mass, adoration, and nearly ever parish event, often accompanied by her affable and talkative grown sons Patrick and Jack. These people knew Jeanne had a deep faith, and wanted to know more about it. Where had that faith come from? How had it sustained her through the loss of a son, her husband, and a daughter? How had it carried her during Patrick's illness and ongoing recovery?

Beyond that, there was the fact that, despite the years that had bent her shoulders and silvered her hair, Jeanne Atkins was clearly a force to be reckoned with. "She started a cheesecake business when she was fifty years old," an acquaintance whispered as we watched Jeanne leaving the chapel one day. Another friend confided, "She used to walk around purposely dropping money for people to find," and still another parishioner shared, "Jeanne was instrumental in starting our adoration chapel. She still provides the beautiful flowers every week."

When fellow Catholic author Beth Leonard introduced us to suggest we work together, Jeanne was not surprised. "A lot of people have told me I should write a book," she said, "but I'm not really sure what they thought I should write about."

When Jeanne and I met to discuss the idea further, Jeanne began to share a few of her stories. They were stories that stood alone and would make for interesting reading: How Jeanne arrived at the idea to start that cheesecake company in the first place; her son Patrick giving money to anyone in need, with no expectation of repayment; Jeanne's admonition of the parish council when they were questioning the need for an adoration chapel, "You would prevent us from adoring Our Lord?!"

What I knew would make for *great* reading – for the Christian, at least – was the way that God was interwoven into every one of those stories. That cheesecake company? Jeanne joined her 200 employees on the factory floor every day to spend time in prayer. Patrick's generous spirit? It was the fruit of a mother who prayed and fasted for 40 days for the health of her daughter Laurie. The commitment to the adoration chapel? That was the outgrowth of a love for Christ in the Eucharist that had developed when she was a young girl in elementary school.

Still, Jeanne wasn't sure. "Do you really think anyone wants to read these stories?" she asked me numerous times. Finally, though, she was ready to take the plunge... on one condition: "If this will bring people closer to God, I want to do it."

The book you're holding in your hands is the outgrowth of that desire. It takes snippets from the stories of Jeanne's life and pairs them with a scripture verse and reflection. It moves in a loosely chronological format, but not rigidly so – enough that I think you'll get a nice overview of Jeanne's life while also learning from her deep devotion to Christ and, I hope, deepening your own. It's a format that allows you to read for a few minutes every day, or for one longer sitting. Regardless of how you go about it, Jeanne and I both hope you'll take time to linger and consider how the scriptures and reflections apply to your own life of faith.

As an author and a bit of a perfectionist, I must note one thing: you'll notice that the heavenly pronouns in the scripture verses are left lower case, while they are upper case in the quotes from Jeanne, and in the reflections. This is because the translation of scripture we've used (New American Bible, Revised Edition) requires that the text be copied exactly, including capitalization and punctuation. Yet, Jeanne and I both agree that God, Christ, and the Holy Spirit deserve a capital "H." So we flew in the face of convention and followed our hearts – where we had license to, at least!

Finally, I believe I can speak (or write, as it were) for both Jeanne and myself when I express this prayer for every reader:

May this book be a blessing to you. May it contribute to your life of faith, drawing you closer to Christ and His love. May it be an instrument in God's hands to help you attain the life of prayer He desires for you; the Trust He longs to receive from you; and the courage He wishes to sustain in you. May you go out and create your own stories of a life lived in close communion with Him!

Yours in Christ,
Stephanie Engelman

Remembering God's Mighty Deeds

Jeanne:

Years ago, I sat on a plane next to two men. They were evangelical Christians, so when they learned I was Catholic, they wanted to save my soul. Then I got to talking. They were hanging on every word, and they told me I should write a book.

I have no idea what their names were, or where they were from, but I wish I could thank them. While many others have encouraged me to write my stories down, those two men were the very first to plant the idea.

To be honest, I've always wondered what they thought I should write about, but if my stories can bring anyone closer to God, I would like to pass them on.

Scripture:

I will recall the deeds of the Lord;
    yes, recall your wonders of old.
I will ponder all your works;
    on your exploits I will meditate.
Your way, God, is holy;
    what god is as great as our God?
You are the God who does wonders;
    among the peoples you have revealed your might.
With your mighty arm you redeemed your people,
    the children of Jacob and Joseph. (Psalm 77:12-16)

Reflection:

When the Jewish people celebrate the Passover each year, they recount the events of the Exodus, in which God freed His chosen people from slavery in Egypt. They do this at the command of God, with an understanding of how very important it is to remember His mighty work in the history of the Israelites.

Has God wrought mighty deeds for you? Write them down!

Proclaim them to others! Remembering the deeds of the Lord will increase your faith, and that of those around you.

If God does not seem to have worked mighty deeds in your life, watch and wait, be patient and pray. Develop your relationship with Him, that you may trust Him and turn to Him in times of doubt, uncertainty, and trouble. You will begin to see His hand in your life.

Let us pray: Lord, today, help me to recall and ponder your mighty works.

Christ in the Eucharist

Jeanne:

My first memory of God is so vivid! I was a little girl at Mass during school. I was surrounded by children, kneeling off to the left of the big church, up near the front.

The priest elevated the Holy Eucharist, and I fell in love with Christ, present in the Eucharist. I knew I never wanted to be apart from Him.

I've gone to daily Mass ever since, and sometimes twice a day. As a young girl, I would wake up early on summer mornings to go to daily Mass with my father. I continued to go as a mother with young children. I don't know how I would have survived all these years without the Eucharist

What an incredible gift God gave me!

Scripture:

"I am the living bread that came down from heaven; whoever eats this bread will live forever; and the bread that I will give is my flesh for the life of the world." (John 6:51)

Reflection:

Many of us are unable to receive Christ in the Eucharist daily, but we are all able to welcome Him into our hearts. How might you welcome Him today?

Let us pray: My Jesus, I believe that Thou art truly present in the Most Holy Sacrament. I love Thee above all things, and I desire to possess Thee within my soul. Since I am unable now to receive Thee sacramentally, come at least spiritually into my heart. I embrace Thee as being already there, and unite myself wholly to Thee; never permit me to be separated from Thee.

The Power of the Eucharist

Jeanne:

Every day, when I walk back from receiving Holy Communion, my prayer is that everyone in that church will somehow know the power of the Holy Eucharist.

Scripture:

Jesus said to them, "Amen, amen, I say to you, unless you eat the flesh of the Son of Man and drink his blood, you do not have life within you. Whoever eats my flesh and drinks my blood has eternal life, and I will raise him on the last day. For my flesh is true food, and my blood is true drink. Whoever eats my flesh and drinks my blood remains in me and I in him. Just as the living Father sent me and I have life because of the Father, so also the one who feeds on me will have life because of me." (John 6:53-57)

Reflection:

We who partake in the Holy Eucharist *remain in Christ*, and Christ *remains in us*. This miracle is visually demonstrated by the single drop of water which the priest intermingles with the wine during Consecration. *We* are the water, *Christ* is the wine, and the two become intermingled. You can neither remove the water from the wine, nor the wine from the water.

Being one with Christ? That's powerful!

Let us pray: Come, Holy Spirit. Help me to know the power of the Holy Eucharist.

Only God...

The whole idea of the Eucharist sounds crazy, but that's what makes me believe in it. Who but God would even think of such a thing? And to give us a gift that gives us strength throughout our lives. Only God would conceive of such a thing!

Scripture:

[Jesus said,] "Just as the living Father sent me and I have life because of the Father, so also the one who feeds on me will have life because of me. This is the bread that came down from heaven. Unlike your ancestors who ate and still died, whoever eats this bread will live forever." ...

Then many of his disciples who were listening said, "This saying is hard; who can accept it?" Since Jesus knew that his disciples were murmuring about this, he said to them, "Does this shock you? What if you were to see the Son of Man ascending to where he was before? It is the spirit that gives life, while the flesh is of no avail. The words I have spoken to you are spirit and life. But there are some of you who do not believe." (John 6:57–58, 60-64)

Reflection:

As Jeanne said, the whole idea of the Eucharist sounds crazy, and many Christians today do not believe that it truly is the Body, Blood, Soul, and Divinity of Christ – even Catholics!

This is nothing new. Disciples walked away from Christ when He proclaimed, "my flesh is true food, and my blood is true drink." (John 6:55) "This saying is hard," they said. "Who can accept it?" But Jesus did not call them back to correct a misunderstanding. Why? Because there was no misunderstanding.

Do you believe that Christ is present in the Eucharist, Body, Blood, Soul, and Divinity? Do you ponder this awesome fact every time you receive the Sacrament?

If you do not believe, what is holding you back?

Let us pray: Lord, I believe. Help my unbelief!

Holy Communion vs. Math and Geometry

<u>Jeanne:</u>

When I was a child, children at Catholic schools went to Mass every day. Today, they go once or twice a week. That's like saying math and geography are more important than Holy Communion. They're not.

I would like you to change that back, God.

<u>Scripture:</u>

Every day they devoted themselves to meeting together in the temple area and to breaking bread in their homes. They ate their meals with exultation and sincerity of heart, praising God and enjoying favor with all the people. And every day the Lord added to their number those who were being saved. (Acts 2:46-47)

<u>Reflection:</u>

The disciples whom Jesus taught directly broke the bread of Communion every day. They did so at great peril, risking life, limb, and family to receive their Eucharistic food.

Do you follow in the disciples' footsteps, or do you only go to Mass when it's an obligation? When you do receive the Eucharist, do you take it for granted, or do you fully appreciate the tremendous gift that it is – Christ's flesh for the life of the world (cf. John 6:51)?

Let us pray: Lord, you are the giver of life and of every good thing. Please help me to place you before everything else in my life. Help me to comprehend the generosity of your gifts, especially the gift of the Eucharist.

The Importance of Priests

Priests have no idea how many lives they touch, and I think that's too bad. I don't know the name of that priest who elevated the Host that day I fell in love with Christ in the Eucharist, but I pray for him and thank God for him often.

Scripture:

Then he took the bread, said the blessing, broke it, and gave it to them, saying, "This is my body, which will be given for you; do this in memory of me." (Luke 22:19)

Reflection:

Our Eucharistic sacrifice can only be offered through the consecrated hands of a priest, who operates in persona Christi (in the person of Christ) so that bread and wine are miraculously transformed into the very flesh and blood of Christ. What an amazing ministry! And yet, that's not the extent of what priests do. They also stand in the person of Christ to hear our confession and offer us reconciliation. They counsel, they marry, they anoint, they baptize, and much more.

What priest has had the greatest impact in your life?

Let us pray: O Jesus, I pray for your faithful and fervent priests;

for your unfaithful and tepid priests;

for your priests laboring at home or abroad in distant mission fields;

for your tempted priests;

for your lonely and desolate priests;

for your young priests;

for your dying priests;

for the souls of your priests in purgatory.

But above all, I recommend to you the priests dearest to me:
the priest who baptized me;
the priests who absolved me from my sins;
the priests at whose Masses I assisted and who gave me your
Body and Blood in Holy Communion;
the priests who taught and instructed me;
all the priests to whom I am indebted in any other
way (especially .....).
O Jesus, keep them all close to your heart,
and bless them abundantly in time and in eternity.
Amen.

(Prayer written by St. Thérèse of Lisieux)

Honoring Our Parents

Jeanne:

I have never met anyone I admired or respected more than my parents. I was the third oldest of eleven children, and all my brothers and sisters would say the same thing. They were just awesome parents.

Scripture:

Honor your father and your mother, that you may have a long life in the land the LORD your God is giving you. (Exodus 20:12)

Reflection:

The command to honor our mothers and fathers appears before "thou shall not murder," "thou shall not commit adultery," and "thou shall not steal." And yet, all too often we witness people – and find ourselves – dis-honoring parents!

In what ways might you honor your parents today? If they have passed, you can pray for their souls. If they are living, you might call them, invite them to dinner, or send a card.

Let us pray: Thank you, Father, for the gift of my earthly parents! Help me to honor them, to love them, and to pray for them.

Marital Bliss

Jeanne:

I remember going down to the City Market in Indianapolis with my father. He would buy the groceries for the week, and he did some of the cooking, as well. My mother was busy taking care of eleven children, so he did that to help her out. He was so thoughtful.

Scripture

So [also] husbands should love their wives as their own bodies. He who loves his wife loves himself. For no one hates his own flesh but rather nourishes and cherishes it, even as Christ does the church, because we are members of his body. (Eph 5:28-30)

Reflection

This scripture is one that makes many in our modern world squirm. Yet, at its foundation is the unquestionable answer to marital bliss: Love one another as you love yourself. Nourish and cherish the other, want the good of the other. If both parties in the marriage will follow this instruction, the marriage will be strong, the home happy, and the family holy.

What can you do today to show your love for your spouse?

Let us pray: Lord Jesus Christ, help me to follow your instruction to love others as I love myself, especially those closest to me.

Christian Obedience

Jeanne:

When my friends started to smoke, I asked my daddy whether he cared if I smoked.

"My dear, I prefer you not."

End of conversation. Instead of ranting and raving, that was it.

Another time, some people suggested that I try out for Miss America. I was excited, of course! I went home and told Daddy.

"My dear, do you really want to parade around in front of hundreds of people in a swimming suit?"

I wanted to say yes. It was my decision. I didn't, of course.

Scripture:

Now, if you obey me completely and keep my covenant, you will be my treasured possession among all peoples, though all the earth is mine. (Exodus 19:5)

Reflection:

Just as Jeanne's father provided loving boundaries for her, so our Father in Heaven provides boundaries for us – the ten commandments and the teachings of Christ, with the guidance of the Church.

Do you attempt to live within the bounds of God's covenant?? How can you do so more fully?

Let us pray: Father, sometimes, I struggle to live within your boundaries. Yet, I know that you gave them to me out of love, so that I might live more fully as your precious child. Please help me to follow your commands, and to seek reconciliation with you when I fail in my attempts to do so.

Think About These Things

My sister Betty was a year older than me. She didn't like school very well, and repeated the first grade, so we went through school together from first grade up. We were in the same grade, but we were very different from one another.

Betty became a religious sister in St. Louis. A few weeks before she died, she called me. "Jeanne, I want you to know that I love you so much. I've always wished I was more like you."

I laughed and I said, "Oh, Betty, that's so funny! I always wished I was more like you!"

Scripture

No more shall you be called "Forsaken,"
  nor your land called "Desolate,"
But you shall be called "My Delight is in her,"
  and your land "Espoused."
For the LORD delights in you,
  and your land shall be espoused.
For as a young man marries a virgin,
  your Builder shall marry you;
And as a bridegroom rejoices in his bride
  so shall your God rejoice in you. (Isa 62:4-5)

Reflection

So often, we compare ourselves to others and believe we fall short. Yet, the Lord delights in us! He rejoices over us!

Do you accept these words as truth? Spend a few minutes meditating on them and accepting them into your heart. The Lord delights in YOU.

Let us pray: Lord, I praise you because I am fearfully and wonderfully made; wonderful are your works! (cf Psa 139:14)

Iron Sharpens Iron

<u>Jeanne:</u>

My sister Joan was the oldest girl. When we were in high school, I saw a dress that I just loved. Joan quit eating lunch and saved her lunch money to help me buy that dress.

Now was I blessed? Could I have asked for more? I don't think so.

<u>Scripture</u>

Iron is sharpened by iron;

one person sharpens another. (Prov. 27:17)

<u>Reflection</u>

Jeanne's blessing was greater than buying a dress she'd fallen in love with. More importantly, she was blessed by the generous example of her older sister, which then encouraged Jeanne to make sacrifices for others throughout her life.

Who are the people in your life who have helped sharpen you in faith? When have you helped sharpen someone else's faith?

Let us pray: Lord God, thank you for the people who have helped to sharpen my faith, that I may follow you more faithfully. Thank you for the opportunity to sharpen the faith of others. Today, help me to be a worthy tool in your loving hands.

The growing Wieck family, circa 1937. Jeanne is second from the right, standing in the white dress.

Memento Mori

Jeanne:

Before he passed, my father wrote a letter to our family. In it, he thanked my mother for all she had done over the years; he thanked his children for living upright and exemplary lives; and he thanked God for giving him the faith, a wonderful wife, and a fine family.[1] He ended with this:

> I remind you that only one thing is necessary, and that is to save your immortal soul. So love one another and help one another, especially if they are in need. Keep the faith, the commandments. May God's choicest blessings be yours and may we meet in eternity.

Scripture:

Therefore, stay awake! For you do not know on which day your Lord will come. Be sure of this; if the master of the house had known the hour of night when the thief was coming, he would have stayed awake and not let his house be broken into. So, too, you also must be prepared, for at an hour you do not expect, the Son of Man will come. (Matt 24:42-44)

Reflection:

The phrase *memento mori* has regained popularity in recent years. The Latin term reminds us, "Remember you will die!" The Church has long-standing tradition, rooted in the teachings of Christ, that we should be mindful of our deaths. Doing so will help us to be more mindful of the way we live our lives.

If you were going to die tomorrow, how would you live differently today?

Let us pray: Lord, help me to live each day as if it might be my last, in loving service to you.

Personal Conduct

Jeanne:

When I was a sophomore in high school, my family moved to Indianapolis from St. Louis. We became parishioners at St. Joan of Arc Parish, and I was involved in the Legion of Mary there. I was at St. Joan of Arc so often, a lot of people thought I went to school there, though in reality I went to St. Agnes, the all-girls high school.

I received quite a few invitations to dances, both at St. Joan of Arc and Cathedral, the all-boys high school. Of course, our dances were all very innocent, instead of what kids do today.

Scripture:

Let no one have contempt for your youth, but set an example for those who believe, in speech, conduct, love, faith, and purity. (1 Tim 4:12)

Reflection:

Times have changed. Whereas Jeanne wore dresses to her high school dances and danced at arms' length from her partner, today's teens wear leggings and bare midriff tops with nary a centimeter keeping partners apart as they gyrate on the dance floor. This does not reflect God's will, but rather a loosening moral code reinforced again and again by the media, retailers, and peers. Yet, the scripture remains the same. We are called to conduct ourselves with love, faith, and purity.

Is this an area in your life which offers room for improvement? Your speech, dress, or conduct? What about your children or grandchildren? How can you make positive steps in this area today?

Let us pray: Lord, help me to set an example for those who believe, in speech, conduct, love, faith, and purity.

Jeanne with her aunts, uncles, and cousins. Jeanne is in the second row from the back, third from the right.

Order vs. Chaos

<u>Jeanne:</u>

There were eight girls and three boys in my family – eleven children! Can you imagine a house with so many children? You'd probably expect that it would have been chaotic, but it was just the opposite, always organized and filled with love. It's hard to believe, but I lived it!

<u>Scripture:</u>

He is not the God of disorder but of peace. (1 Cor 14:33)

<u>Reflection:</u>

Jeanne's parent's ability to create a home filled with love serves as a reminder that peace is possible, even in the midst of the busyness and competing priorities of a large family. When life feels out of control, let us remember that in the beginning, the spirit of God moved over the chaos (Gen 1). By His simple command, light was made, the firmament established, the waters gathered together, and the dry land appeared.

When does life tend to feel most chaotic to you? Consider praying in advance of those situations whenever you can.

Let us pray: Lord, today, I turn the chaos and disorder of my life over to you and ask for your help. Please bring order and peace into my life and family.

Love One Another

Jeanne:

I was out to lunch one day and my friend said, "I always hated my brother." I nearly fell off my chair. That's so tragic! How could you hate your brother?

My family would always do anything for each other. When Patrick fell on the ice and broke his foot, my two living sisters, Mary Dee and Connie Jo, and my brother-in-law, Tom Murphy, drove to Indianapolis from St. Louis to visit him. Going from St. Louis to Indianapolis and back in a single day is a challenge, but that's how my family was.

Scripture:

"I give you a new commandment: love one another. As I have loved you, so you also should love one another. This is how all will know that you are my disciples, if you have love for one another." (John 13:34-35)

Reflection:

Let us pray: Lord Jesus, there are those in my life who I sometimes feel don't "deserve" my love. And yet, I'm forced to recognize that I don't "deserve" your love, either. I have sinned against you. I have failed to love you as I ought. I have taken you for granted and injured those you love. Still, you love me. In fact, there's nothing I can do which would make you stop loving me.

Please help me to love [fill in the blank] as you love me, even though they may not "deserve" it, because you love me, even when I don't "deserve" it.

Serving the Lord

I had four aunts who were consecrated religious, and we went to the convent to visit them often. Two of my sisters became consecrated religious as well, joining the school sisters of Notre Dame. I never considered it, though. I spent one weekend down at their retreat center, and I remember thinking, *On a Saturday night, you have to go to bed at nine o'clock?* That sounded awful to me at the time! Now, it sounds wonderful!

Scripture:

There are different kinds of spiritual gifts but the same Spirit; there are different forms of service but the same Lord; there are different workings but the same God who produces all of them in everyone. (1 Cor 12:4-6)

Reflection:

Each of us is called to serve the Lord in some way. Jeanne's service was as a wife and mother, a friend, an inspiring example, and, eventually, as a business woman who would found a company to help her son Tom and provide meaningful employment to a community.

How are you called to serve the Lord? How can you do that, in a better and more meaningful way, today than you did yesterday?

Let us pray: Father, today, help me to use my gifts in service to you.

Seek What is Above

Jeanne:

My mother and dad had season tickets to Notre Dame football for years. I went up there often, and it was a lot of fun. On one occasion, I remember going up with my girlfriends when I was in business school. Three of us girls went up the night before for a dance, and then to the football game the next day. Our tickets were across the stadium from the boys, and we all sat and watched that game in the bitter cold. We were half-frozen to death, so, finally, we left the game, went to the boys' dorm, and crawled in the bed to get warm. When the boys found out, they said they would have been expelled. Can you imagine? In today's world, no one would think twice about that!

Scripture:

If then you were raised with Christ, seek what is above, where Christ is seated at the right hand of God. Think of what is above, not of what is on earth. For you have died, and your life is hidden with Christ in God. When Christ your life appears, then you too will appear with him in glory. Put to death, then, the parts of you that are earthly: immorality, impurity, passion, evil desire, and the greed that is idolatry. (Col 3:1-5)

Reflection:

We live in a world where virtue is much-maligned and self-control applies more to working out and eating right than to keeping the ten commandments. Yet God's Word and commands are unchanging. Regardless of what has become "normal" in the world, we are called to purity and holiness, to build lives centered upon Christ, that we may know and glorify Him for all eternity.

Has the "normal" of the world crept into your way of thinking or living?

Let us pray: Heavenly Father, you do not change. Please help me to see the world through the light of your Word, and help me to be an instrument of change to bring your creation back to you.

Whom Will You Serve?

<u>Jeanne:</u>

One time, a few years after my parents had passed, I said to my husband, "Tom, do you miss your parents like I miss mine?" He responded, "No. I miss yours."

That says a lot about my parents, but I always felt that he married me as much for my family and the strength he saw in them as he married *me*.

<u>Scripture:</u>

...choose today whom you will serve, the gods your ancestors served beyond the River or the gods of the Amorites in whose country you are dwelling. As for me and my household, we will serve the LORD. (Josh 24:15)

<u>Reflection:</u>

The strength Tom recognized in Jeanne's family was surely rooted in its members' deep devotion and service to the Lord.

Does your family possess the same commitment and strength? What worldly "gods" might be an obstacle on the path toward perfect service to the One and Only God?

Let us pray: Lord, today, help me to love and serve you with all my heart, mind, and soul.

The True Church

<u>Jeanne:</u>

Tom was raised a non-Catholic Christian, but he converted to Catholicism before he even asked me to marry him. His grandmother was so horrified, she sent her minister – not once, but three times! – to try to talk him out of doing this "awful" thing.

You reach people through kindness and a great deal of prayer, though, and Tom's grandmother and I ultimately became very close. Before she died, she called me. She told me that she wanted me to know that I was the best thing that ever happened to Tom.

Tom grew very close to God later in his life. I would wake at night and find him praying the Rosary. I'm so glad he came to appreciate his faith, and I hope everyone will develop a close relationship with God.

<u>Scripture:</u>

"And so I say to you, you are Peter, and upon this rock I will build my church, and the gates of the netherworld shall not prevail against it." (Matt 16:18)

<u>Reflection:</u>

Many families face deep divisions over matters of faith.

Is your family one of these? How might you begin to bridge the divide today?

Let us pray: Heavenly Father, unite your people. May we be of one heart and one mind, in love and service to you.

The Gift of Faith

<u>Jeanne:</u>

When the children were little, I would bring all five of them to daily Mass with me, and I'm sure I looked hysterical. My son Patrick used to say, "Mother, faith is the greatest gift you gave us. You didn't preach at us, you showed us."

That's the most important part, the greatest gift we can give anyone. Faith. People have no idea what strength they can get from that. I would not have survived what I've had to live through these last fourteen years without the gift of faith.

<u>Scripture:</u>

I have the strength for everything through him who empowers me. (Phil 4:13)

<u>Reflection:</u>

Christ tells us that, with faith, we can move mountains (cf. Matt 21:21, Mark 11:23). But He also tells us that, to achieve such results, we must truly believe it will be done.

Do you have faith like that, free from any doubts or limitations?

Let us pray: Lord, please give me a faith that will move mountains. Remove all my doubts, that I may trust fully in your awesome and limitless power.

God's Plan

<u>Jeanne:</u>

My son Jack nearly died three times. On one of those occasions, his leg touched a power line when he was climbing a tree. Forty thousand volts of electricity coursed through his body. The doctors and nurses all agreed: the fact that he survived was a miracle.

Jack says he knows God's going to use him for something, and I believe he's right. In fact, a few years ago, four different people came to my door. Two I knew, two I didn't. Every one of them told me what a remarkable difference Jack had made in their lives. One of them had five children, and said, "We wouldn't have had Christmas if it hadn't been for Jack."

<u>Scripture:</u>

We are his handiwork, created in Christ Jesus for the good works that God has prepared in advance, that we should live in them. (Eph 2:10)

<u>Reflection:</u>

God has a plan for each and every one of us, but in order for Him to use us in that plan, we must cooperate fully, seeking His Holy Will in every moment of our lives.

What decisions will you make today? Perhaps it's the way in which you use your free time, the way you respond to others, or the way you care for yourself or your surroundings. Will you consider what God's Will is in these things?

Let us pray: Father in Heaven, I know that, when I seek your good and holy Will, peace and joy will follow. Please show me your Will in the decisions I make, and help me to always act upon it.

Never Too Late to Pray

<u>Jeanne:</u>

The children were young, and we were buzzing down Illinois St. in a hurry to get to noon Mass at a church downtown. All of a sudden I heard sirens. I was so upset, because I had just gotten two tickets in the last few months. I was horrified.

After the officer left, I started driving again, and I was crying. It was my third ticket, and I knew I could lose my license. My two little girls, Lisa and Laurie, were hanging on the seat from the back, and they peaked over and said, "Mommy, it's okay, it's okay. We're praying really hard it will be okay."

When I went to court, the judge called me up. "Can your family afford this in their monthly budget?" he asked.

"No."

"And how many children do you have?"

"Five."

"I assume you need your car to take them places?"

"Yes, sir, I do."

Would you believe, I walked out of there with no court costs and no fine? Those little girls were praying that their mother would get out of trouble, and she did.

It's never too late to pray.

<u>Scripture:</u>

He is before all things, and in him all things hold together. (Col 1:17)

<u>Reflection:</u>

It's never too soon to pray, and never too late to pray. Nothing is too big, and nothing is too small. God is in control. He controls everything, and He cares about every detail.

What will you pray for today?

Divided Christianity

Jeanne:

When Tom got transferred, we moved to an area that was very anti-Catholic. I remember a woman coming up to me, so friendly and nice, and she knew by my accent that I was new in town. She introduced herself, asked where my husband worked, how many children I had, and where I lived. And then she asked what church I belonged to. I said, "St. Andrews Catholic," and it was like a door shut in my face. She was gone.

It didn't bother me, but I think of all the things that have caused our beloved God pain, the separation of Christians is one of the greatest. I wish that all the different groups were more tolerant of one another.

Scripture:

I urge you, brothers, in the name of our Lord Jesus Christ, that all of you agree in what you say, and that there be no divisions among you, but that you be united in the same mind and in the same purpose. (1 Col 1:10)

Reflection:

Our witness to other Christians is an important one, and vital to restoring Christian unity.

Do you proudly proclaim your faith? If not, what is holding you back?

Let us pray: Come Holy Spirit. Unite your people. Spread the effect of grace of your flame of love over all humanity.

(Prayer adapted from *The Spiritual Diary of Elizabeth Kindelmann*)

Fractured Relationships

<u>Jeanne:</u>

A young man used to cover the adoration shift from one to two in the morning, just before my shift. He told me that he was a direct relative of Martin Luther, and that the whole family was horrified when Martin Luther left the Church. Not one family member followed him, the young man said. Isn't that amazing?

I believe Martin Luther was led by the sin of pride. How could you think you're more important than God and start your own religion? That had to cause God so much pain.

<u>Scripture:</u>

Where do the wars and where do the conflicts among you come from? Is it not from your passions that make war within your members? You covet but do not possess. You kill and envy but you cannot obtain; you fight and wage war. You do not possess because you do not ask. You ask but do not receive, because you ask wrongly, to spend it on your passions. (James 4:1-3)

<u>Reflection:</u>

Martin Luther's response to the problems he saw within the Church hierarchy was to divorce the Church and found his own religion. Divorce, Jesus tells us, is caused by hardness of hearts, further admonishing that one who divorces his wife and marries another commits adultery. (cf Matt 19:8,9) Surely, the better response on Luther's part would have been to pray for the Church, and trust in the goodness of God to correct that which was wrong?

Is there a fractured relationship in your own life that needs your trust-filled prayer?

Let us pray: Father, bless your Holy Church. Please heal every broken relationship, both between Christian communities and also within my own life.

Child-Proof

Shortly before we moved back to Indiana from Virginia, our daughter Laurie began to act strangely. She was very depressed, and had started isolating herself from the family in a very worrisome way. She wasn't Laurie anymore, and we couldn't figure out where our beloved daughter had gone.

When I took her to a well-regarded psychiatrist, he deemed her a danger to herself, and declared that she needed to be put into an asylum.

I wasn't about to place my daughter in an asylum hundreds of miles away from where we would be living! And so I told him, "We're moving back to Indianapolis. I'll take her to a doctor there."

"Oh, but she could jump out of the car," the doctor argued. "It won't be safe for her."

"She can't jump out of the car. We have a brand-new car, but the back doors are already broken. We can't unlock them. We'll just wait to get it fixed once we're in Indianapolis."

Little did we know, the doors weren't broken at all. Our new car was equipped with all the latest and greatest in safety equipment – including child-proof locks!

Scripture:

My God will fully supply whatever you need, in accord with his glorious riches in Christ Jesus. (Phil 4:18)

Reflection:

The Lord fully understands our needs, even before we do. He will invariably provide exactly what we need, even when we don't know what that is. While Jeanne would have preferred a quick and easy "healing" of her daughter, God had other plans.

Nonetheless, He provided what the Atkins family needed at the time – a way to get their daughter safely home, in order to gain more time to pray and discern what they should do next.

When has the Lord answered a prayer in a way you did not expect?

Let us pray: Father, I may never know the many ways in which you've answered my prayers. Thank you for your wise and mysterious ways.

The Atkins family, circa 2005

Expert Advice

Jeanne:

Once we got Laurie safely back to Indianapolis, I told God I would pray and fast for 40 days for her healing. After 40 days of fasting on bread and water, I received a message from God: *Take her off the medicine.*

Tom worked for a pharmaceutical giant, so the idea that medications were causing Laurie's troubles was not going to be a popular one with him. I called him at work and said, "Honey, I got a message loud and clear that we need to take Laurie off all her medication."

"Oh, honey, we can't do that."

Ten minutes later, though, he called me back. "Honey, you have been fasting and praying so hard, if you feel led to take her off the medications, you go ahead and do that."

We took her off, and she was never sick like that again.

Scripture:

Jesus, on seeing a crowd rapidly gathering, rebuked the unclean spirit and said to it, "Mute and deaf spirit, I command you: come out of him and never enter him again!" Shouting and throwing the boy into convulsions, it came out. He became like a corpse, which caused many to say, "He is dead!" But Jesus took him by the hand, raised him, and he stood up. When he entered the house, his disciples asked him in private, "Why could we not drive it out?" He said to them, "This kind can only come out through prayer and fasting." (Mark 9:25-29)

Reflection:

Worldly experts rarely see prayer and fasting as a solution to problems, but we know that some ailments are healed only through these two things. While the traditional fast is bread and water, God is honored through every fast, including things like giving up television for a day, skipping dessert, or leaving the salt off your food.

For what intention might you pray and fast today?

Let us pray: Lord, help me to remember and be strengthened by the power of prayer and fasting.

Life in the Barn

Jeanne:

When we moved back to Indiana, we lived in a farm house in Carmel for about three years before turning the barn into a home. I've never regretted it. It's been a lot of fun, and we've loved it. It's great for house guests, and great for parties. We've had line dances in the loft, and we have a huge bedroom upstairs for all six granddaughters, plus a small one we call "the nook" for the two grandsons.

Scripture:

She wrapped him in swaddling clothes and laid him in a manger, because there was no room for them in the inn. (Luke 2:7)

Reflection:

The fact that Jesus was born in a stable reminds us that it doesn't matter how luxurious or humble our homes are. What matters is that we use our homes – and all our possessions – to glorify God. We may do so through quality time spent with family, or by opening our doors to a prayer group or someone in need. We may simply do so by creating a home that is peaceful and filled with love, intentionally seeking to emulate that of the Holy Family.

How might God be calling you to glorify Him through your worldly goods today?

Let us pray: Thank you, Father, for your every blessing. Help me to use all you have given me for your greater glory.

Accomplish More

People used to ask me how I accomplished so much. I always said, "The more I pray, the more I accomplish."

Scripture:

Blessed is the man who does not walk
  in the counsel of the wicked,
Nor stand in the way of sinners,
  nor sit in company with scoffers.
Rather, the law of the Lord is his joy;
  and on his law he meditates day and night.
He is like a tree
  planted near streams of water,
  that yields its fruit in season;
Its leaves never wither;
  whatever he does prospers. (Psalm 1:1-3)

Reflection:

A popular quote attributed to St. Francis de Sales says, "Every one of us needs half an hour of prayer every day, except when we are busy – then we need an hour." In following this advice, Jeanne found that, rather than losing time to prayer, she gained time through prayer! Prayer helps us stay centered on that which is more important. When we keep Christ at the center, we are promised that everything we do will prosper!

Do you sometimes feel you're too busy to pray? How might you take this Jeanne's experience, and God's words, to heart?

Let us pray: Father in heaven, help me to meditate on your law day and night, that you may prosper all my works.

The Shepherd's Voice

Jeanne:

I have found that if I talk to God a lot, I get answers very directly.

Scripture:

Whoever enters through the gate is the shepherd of the sheep. The gatekeeper opens it for him, and the sheep hear his voice, as he calls his own sheep by name and leads them out. When he has driven out all his own, he walks ahead of them, and the sheep follow him, because they recognize his voice. (John 10:2-4)

Reflection:

Talking to God and listening for His responses is essential to Christian discipleship. His answers may come through Scripture, through other Christians, through signs, and – yes! – even through a quiet voice in our heads. When we are in relationship with God, we are able to test and discern when He is truly speaking. We know the voice of our Shepherd.

Spend a few minutes in silence, listening for the voice of the Lord.

Let us pray: Speak, Lord. Your servant is listening.

Attitude

This is one of my favorite quotes, from Charles R. Swindoll:

> The longer I live, the more I realize the impact of attitude on life. Attitude, to me, is more important than facts. It is more important than the past, than education, than money, than circumstances, than failures, than successes, than what other people think or say or do. It is more important than appearance, giftedness, or skill. It will make or break a company...a church...a home. The remarkable thing is we have a choice every day regarding the attitude we will embrace for that day. We cannot change our past...we cannot change the fact that people will act in a certain way. We cannot change the inevitable. The only thing we can do is play on the one string we have, and that is our attitude...I am convinced that life is 10% what happens to me and 90% how I react to it. And so it is with you...we are in charge of our own attitudes.

Scripture:

Finally, brothers, whatever is true, whatever is honorable, whatever is just, whatever is pure, whatever is lovely, whatever is gracious, if there is any excellence and if there is anything worthy of praise, think about these things. (Phil 4:8)

Reflection:

If we follow the advice of St. Paul in Philippians 4:8, we are sure to have excellent attitudes. Focus on the positive and, regardless of what happens, we will react with grace and strength.

What situation might you face today that will test your positive attitude?

Let us pray: Lord, purify my mind, that I may ponder that which is honorable, pure, lovely, gracious, excellent, and worthy of praise.

Don't Give God the Leftovers

Jeanne:

Another favorite quote is this: "Don't give God the leftovers." There's an order to life: God, family, job.

Scripture:

But seek first the kingdom [of God] and his righteousness, and all these things will be given you besides. (Matt 6:33)

Reflection:

Life isn't about fitting God into the busy-ness. It's about fitting the busy-ness around the God who gave us every good thing. Sometimes that means removing some of the busy-ness. It never means removing God.

Yet, often we find ourselves saying, "I'd pray the Rosary every day, but it takes too long." Or, "I'd go to daily Mass more often, but it's hard to fit into my schedule." Or, "I'd take on a regular holy hour, but I'm just afraid to commit."

Do any of these sound familiar?

Let us pray: Father, help me to remove any busy-ness that is preventing me from spending time with you.

The Wedding Feast of the Lamb

Jeanne:

At one time, I was a new member on the board of a Catholic retreat house in Indiana. I stayed overnight at the retreat house for the board meeting, and I just assumed we would begin our day with the Mass. I left my room in the morning, headed to the chapel, and found the priest sitting there alone.

"What time is the Mass, Father?" I asked.

"They've decided not to have one," he informed me. "They said they were going to have a 'more meaningful service.'"

I was astonished. A more meaningful service than the Mass with the Holy Eucharist? There's no such thing! Apparently, the man running the retreat house didn't know anything about the Holy Eucharist!

I always say what I think, where my God is concerned, as long as He gives me the strength. "Well, Father," I said, "I don't need breakfast. Tell them I went to the parish down the road, and I'll be back. I don't want to miss the Holy Eucharist today."

Scripture:

Then the angel said to me, "Write this: Blessed are those who have been called to the wedding feast of the Lamb." And he said to me, "These words are true; they come from God." (Rev 19:9)

Reflection:

When we hear the priest proclaim these familiar words from Revelation during the Eucharistic prayer, we are reminded that we are responding to an invitation to a wedding feast. Moreover, as Dr. Edward Sri says, "at this great marriage feast, you are no ordinary guest. When you come down the aisle to receive Holy Communion, you come as the bride, as a member of the Church. And you come to be united with your divine Bridegroom who gives Himself to you in the most intimate way possible here on earth – in the Holy Eucharist."[2]

This wedding feast is, as the Catechism tells us, "the source and summit of Christian life." (CCC 1324) Indeed, as Jeanne said, there is no greater or more meaningful service!

Let us pray: Thank you, Jesus, for inviting me to your wedding feast! Thank you for allowing me to be united with you, the divine Bridegroom!

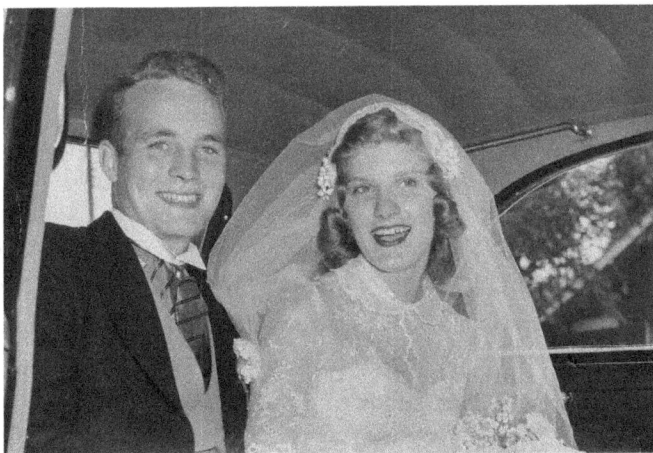

Following a very "meaningful service," the newlyweds Mr. & Mrs. Tom Atkins, June 16, 1951

A Whole Book of Letters

<u>Jeanne:</u>

I used to look up to the Lord and say, "Lord, do I have to learn everything the hard way? Couldn't you just write me a letter?"

And then, one day, I heard Him say, "My dear, I wrote you a whole book of letters."

It was there all the time. I needed to read the Bible!

<u>Scripture:</u>

Do not let this book of the law depart from your lips. Recite it by day and by night, that you may carefully observe all that is written in it; then you will attain your goal; then you will succeed. (Josh 1:8)

<u>Reflection:</u>

"In the sacred books, the Father who is in heaven comes lovingly to meet his children, and talks with them." (CCC 104)

God has written you a whole book of letters. Will you invite Him to talk to you through Sacred Scripture today?

Let us pray: Father, speak to me in your Word today.

Keeping Watch

Jeanne:

A group of us wanted to start a perpetual adoration chapel at my parish, but some of the parish council really pushed back on the idea. When our priest asked me to speak to them during a meeting, I went gladly, bringing along some friends to pray while I was talking.

"You know, I find this absolutely amazing," I told the council. "We have a good, holy pope. He is in support of perpetual adoration. We have a good bishop. He is for perpetual adoration. And we have a good and holy pastor, who wants perpetual adoration. And you people? You would prevent us from adoring our God?"

They voted, and we won.

Scripture:

When he returned to his disciples he found them asleep. He said to Peter, "So you could not keep watch with me for one hour?" (Matt 26:40)

Reflection:

Invariably, parishes report radical changes within their communities when perpetual adoration is established. Faith abounds, sin abates, and vocations boom. Regular adorers report the same in their own lives – an abundance of graces, and a renewal and strengthening of their relationship with Christ.

Do you make a regular holy hour of adoration? If you do, what graces have you received? If you do not, what is holding you back?

Let us pray: Lord, help me to stay with you and remain with you, to watch, and to pray.

Entrust Your Works to the Lord

Jeanne:

We were in Michigan one time on a ski trip with three other couples. Each of us contributed to the meal, and I was responsible for dessert. But when dinner was over, everyone said they were too full to eat the cheesecake I'd made.

"You don't have to be a member of the clean plate club," I told them. "The cheesecake is already plated. Eat what you want." It wasn't long before everyone was nearly licking their plates clean!

I had been praying for a way to help our oldest son, Tom, who was going through a difficult time. I said to my friend Mary Jane, "Do you think it would be crazy if we started a cheesecake company?"

We started with hand mixers, and we kept selling and selling, more and more cheesecakes. At Christmas time, we sent darling Christmas postcards out to advertise that we would deliver the cheesecakes, beautifully gift-wrapped. I spent my entire Advent making bows!

The company grew and grew. We bought land and built a plant, and ultimately the plant tripled in size. We shipped cheesecakes all over the world.

Scripture:

Entrust your works to the LORD, and your plans will succeed. (Prov 16:3)

Reflection:

Jeanne didn't start a company out of greed or avarice, but to help her son during a difficult time. Based upon the way in which she lived the rest of her life, we can rest assured that she trusted her efforts to the Lord, and He did, indeed, bring the Atkins Cheesecake Company great success.

What work are you currently undertaking?

Let us pray: Lord, I offer my work to for your glory. Help me to move forward in faith, trusting that you will, indeed, bring prosperity to my plans, according to your Holy Will.

WHEREAS:	The U.S. Small Business Administration named Atkins International, locally known as Atkins Elegant Desserts, the 2006 State of Indiana Family-Owned Business of the Year; and
WHEREAS:	Atkins Elegant Desserts was established in 1981 by Jeanne Atkins and her son Tom Jr. and later joined by her son Patrick; and
WHEREAS:	Atkins currently has a 70,000+ sq. foot facility with the capacity to double in size allowing for the current production of more than 300 varieties of desserts which are shipped all over the United States, Canada, Europe and more; and
WHEREAS:	A basic business tenant from inception has been that, "There is an order to life; God, family and business." as stated by Jeanne who's motto from the beginning was "Prayer and Perseverance" to which Patrick added "Prayer Perseverance and Perspiration"; and
WHEREAS:	Atkins Elegant Desserts is one of the largest private employers in the City of Noblesville; and
WHEREAS:	The Atkins family represents a tireless dedication to our community, to their employees, and serving as a shining example of the entrepreneurial spirit that has made our community strong; and
WHEREAS:	The City of Noblesville takes pride in the Atkins family's leadership of and willingness to make positive changes in countless lives and a lasting impact on our community.

NOW, THEREFORE, I, John Ditslear, Mayor of the City of Noblesville, of the State of Indiana, do hereby call upon all citizens to recognize Tuesday, April 25th 2006 as "Atkins Elegant Desserts Day" in the City of Noblesville and call upon all citizens to recognize this exceptionally outstanding family business for their contributions and service to the citizens of Noblesville and toward the betterment of our City. We congratulate the Atkins Family and honor them for their faith, hard work and dedication to family values.

IN WITNESS WHEREOF I, John Ditslear, have hereunto set my hand and caused to be affixed the official seal of the City of Noblesville, State of Indiana on this 25th day of April, 2006.

_____
John Ditslear, Mayor

A proclamation from the City of Noblesville, declaring April 25th, 2006 "Atkins Elegant Desserts Day," after the company was named Indiana's Family-Owned Business of the Year. The proclamation cites the family's dedication to the community and their employees, commitment to prayer, & example of the entrepreneurial spirit.

Who, Me, God?

Jeanne:

When I went out into the plant one day, I sensed deep pain within two different people. I felt so badly for them. I learned that the wife of one of the men had just left him and their two children. The other man's father had been taken to jail.

I went back to my office and I prayed, "God, please let them know that you're there for them. They need you desperately."

Then I heard a voice that said, "Why don't you let them know?"

"Who, me, God?"

"Yes."

So I got up out of my chair, and I rushed down the hall. "God, we'd better hurry," I said. "I'm afraid I'll change my mind."

Once I arrived in the plant, I said, "You know, I just feel like we all need prayer in our lives. No one needs to pray if they don't want to, but I feel it would be good if we took time out of the day for this." So we started prayer time. No one had to come, but almost everyone did.

Years later, I went to a funeral for someone from the plant and a man came up to me. "Mrs. Atkins," he said, "I just wanted you to know that after you started prayer time, my dad quit doing drugs, and he was the best father I ever could have had."

Prayer is powerful. It makes a difference.

Scripture:

Have no anxiety at all, but in everything, by prayer and petition, with thanksgiving, make your requests known to God. (Phil 4:6)

Reflection:

When we lift all our joys and trials up to God, we learn something powerful: He will take care of everything. It might not be in exactly the way we expect, but it *will* be exactly what we need.

Let us pray: Jesus, I surrender myself to you. Take care of everything!

O Holy Spirit, Soul
of my soul, I adore Thee.
Enlighten, guide, strengthen
and console me.
Tell me what I ought to do
and command me to do it.
I promise to be submissive
in everything Thou permittest
to happen to me—
only show me
what is Thy will.
Thank You for this new day.

One of Jeanne's favorite prayers, she ran copies of
it and gave it to everyone at the plant.

God Hears

Jeanne:

I was driving home one day and I said, "Lord, I have been praying for my husband to quit smoking, and you haven't done anything about that yet."

When I arrived home and walked into the house, Tom said, "Do you notice anything different about me?"

I looked him up and down and said, "No."

"I had my last cigarette at 4 o'clock."

I remember looking at the clock the moment I said that prayer to God. It was 4 o'clock, exactly.

Isn't that a riot?! But it's the truth.

Scripture:

And we have this confidence in him, that if we ask anything according to his will, he hears us. (1 John 5:14)

Reflection:

God hears every prayer, but we must believe that He can and will answer us. We must also trust that His Will is better than our will.

What prayers have you offered up, which are still unanswered?

Let us pray: Father, please provide the gift of trust, that I might ask with confidence. Please provide the gift of peace, that I might accept your Will over my own.

A Time for Everything

<u>Jeanne:</u>

Our son Patrick always excelled at every sport. He was very smart, and everyone just loved him. He was an excellent salesman for our company, and he traveled the world selling cheesecakes. We had a great relationship.

And then he suffered an aneurism, and a stroke after that. Now, he lives with a severe brain injury. Patrick is still fun to be around, though, and we all just love him. He loves God, and I know God has a very special love for him.

<u>Scripture:</u>

Weeping bitterly, mourning fully,
    pay your tribute of sorrow, as deserved:
A day or two, to prevent gossip;
    then compose yourself after your grief.
For grief can bring on death,
    and heartache can sap one's strength. (Sir 38:17)

<u>Reflection:</u>

Jeanne rightly mourned what had happened to her son, to herself, and to her family. Rather than becoming mired in her sorrow, however, Jeanne followed the advice of Sirach. She focused on the positive, continuing to recognize the blessing of her son.

Let us pray: Father, difficult times will, inevitably, come. When the time for mourning has ended, please provide the strength to compose myself and continue to live the life you want me to live.

The hours we spend with Jesus in the Blessed Sacrament are the nearest thing to heaven for us. During the time spent in adoration we allow God to touch us; we open ourselves to Him; we surrender to Him; we hear His words of love; we respond. Adoration affords us the opportunity to become quiet , quiet enough to hear what His Spirit is saying, and calm enough to reflect upon the deeper meaning of experience, in order to learn what God wants to reveal to us through persons and events in our lives. In adoration we express our dependence on God and our gratitude for all that His love has provided for our salvation, especially for the gift of His living presence in the Blessed Sacrament

"Behold I am with you always, even until the end of time."

Eucharistic Adoration

"Could you not watch one hour with me?"   **Matt. 26:40**

ANGEL'S PRAYER

With the Blessed Sacrament suspended in the air, the angel at Fatima prostrated himself, and recited this prayer:

• *O Most Holy Trinity, Father, Son and Holy Spirit, I adore Thee profoundly. I offer Thee the precious Body, Blood, Soul and Divinity of Jesus Christ, present in all the tabernacles of the world, in reparation for the outrages, sacrileges and indifference by which He is offended. By the infinite merits of the Sacred Heart of Jesus and the Immaculate Heart of Mary, I beg the conversion of poor sinners.*

FOR SOMEONE SPECIAL

Jeanne & Patrick

A holy hour has been made, for all your intentions which are dear to your heart.

BLESSINGS FROM

Rita Whalley

DATE *May-18-16*

PLACE *St. Lukes*

PERPETUAL ADORATION...
JESUS WANTS IT!!!!

A prayer card sent by a dear friend

The Value of Kindness

Jeanne:

Tom and I flew down to Atlanta to be with Patrick, but we were only allowed to visit him for ten minutes at a time. I spent a lot of time in the waiting room. It was a big room, filled with other people whose family members were seriously ill. After a couple of days, I noticed that the room was filled with beautiful bouquets of flowers. I thought I'd better get up and see if any of them were for Patrick. I could hardly believe it. There were 40 bouquets, and every single one was for Patrick. He was an international salesman, so they came from people all over the world: England, France, the United States…

One day, a woman from one of our suppliers called me. After she introduced herself, she said, "I just want you to know, it takes me 45 minutes to drive to work, and I pray for Patrick the whole way." I thought that was so dear.

The priest at the church near the hospital got to know us, and he included Patrick by name in the Mass intentions each day.

There are so many kind people in the world, and their kindness meant more to us than they'll ever know.

Scripture:

Kindness is like a garden of blessings, and almsgiving endures forever. (Sir 41:17, RSV translation)

Reflection:

It is not only the recipient of an act of kindness who is blessed, but also the giver.

Resolve, today, to perform at least one act of kindness.

Let us pray: Too often, Lord, I have seen a need and failed to respond. Please bless me with an opportunity for kindness today.

Spiritual Bouquets

Jeanne:

When we were children in grade school, we used to give our parents spiritual bouquets for Christmas, and I think that was wonderful. I do that for many people, still today.

When Patrick became ill, two of my friends sent me the most beautiful spiritual bouquet. They gave me 30 Rosaries, 25 Masses, 5+ visits to the Blessed Sacrament, 150 ejaculatory prayers, 15 Chaplets of Divine Mercy, 35 novenas to St. Therese of Lisieux, and 10 chaplets to Our Lady of Sorrows.

They sent that to me while Tom and I were staying in the hotel in Atlanta, while Patrick was in the hospital. How incredibly kind, that they would promise to offer so many prayers for us!

Scripture:

They came bringing to him a paralytic carried by four men. Unable to get near Jesus because of the crowd, they opened up the roof above him. After they had broken through, they let down the mat on which the paralytic was lying. When Jesus saw their faith, he said to the paralytic, "Child, your sins are forgiven." (Mark 2:3-5)

Reflection:

Our intercessory prayers can be incredibly powerful!

Who needs your prayer today? Who have you promised to pray for... and forgotten? To whom can you send a spiritual bouquet?

Let us pray: Lord, please hear the prayers all my family, friends, colleagues, and associates. Bless them abundantly and draw them ever closer into your love.

Trying to Forgive

Jeanne:

It was a long time after the aneurism before Patrick was finally able to talk. When he could, we started saying the Our Father together.

Patrick could say the whole prayer, but he changed one thing. He would say, "Forgive us our trespasses, as we _try_ to forgive those who trespass against us."

I laugh at that every time I think of it, but it's true, isn't it? It's hard to forgive people, but we have to try.

Scripture:

"If you forgive others their transgressions, your heavenly Father will forgive you. But if you do not forgive others, neither will your Father forgive your transgressions." (Matt 6:14)

Reflection:

No matter how a person has wronged you, forgiveness is vital to your own emotional and spiritual well-being. If there's someone in your life whom you struggle to forgive, ask God for the grace to try to forgive. If your immediate response to that suggestion is, "But I don't want to try to forgive them," you are not alone! Very often, the first step in forgiving is to ask God for the grace to _want_ to try to forgive. Start there.

Let us pray: Lord God, help me to forgive quickly and generously.

Eye Has Not Seen

<u>Jeanne:</u>

In 2003, Tom, Senior became very ill with cancer of the esophagus. They said he wouldn't survive, but he lived another four years.

I had always told him that I got to die first, and it made me so mad that he got to go before me. Finally, though, he was suffering so terribly that I said, "Honey, you can let go. It's fine with me."

He died while I slept that night, lying in bed next to him.

<u>Scripture:</u>

"What eye has not seen, and ear has not heard,
and what has not entered the human heart,
what God has prepared for those who love him..." (1 Col 2:9)

<u>Reflection:</u>

Having been graced with a glimpse of heaven, St. Maria Faustina wrote, "I saw its inconceivable beauties and the happiness that awaits us after death. I saw how all creatures give ceaseless praise and glory to God. I saw how great is happiness in God, which spreads to all creatures, making them happy...

"This source of happiness is unchanging in its essence, but it is always new, gushing forth happiness for all creatures. Now I understand Saint Paul, who said, "Eye has not seen, nor has ear heard, nor has it entered into the heart of man what God has prepared for those who love Him." (Diary of St. Maria Faustina, 777)

Today, spend a few moments meditating on heaven as St. Faustina describes it.

Let us pray: Father, when my days on earth are through, please welcome me into your heavenly kingdom, that I may praise and glorify you for all eternity.

Walk Humbly with Christ

<u>Jeanne:</u>

All my life, I've been so blessed. I've had such a good life. And then our son Tom Jr. died, and then Patrick suffered the aneurism and stroke. A few years later, Tom Sr. died. A month after that, we learned that our daughter Laurie had cancer, and had a few months to live.

It's been a rough, rough time, but I'm glad God chose me to walk with Him. I think of Christ carrying His cross, and I imagine I'm walking right beside Him, carrying mine. I ask God to help me hold His hand and walk with Him and help Him carry some of His pain.

He's been good to me. Even though I've had a lot of pain, I am humbly grateful.

<u>Scripture:</u>

Then Jesus said to his disciples, "Whoever wishes to come after me must deny himself, take up his cross, and follow me." (Matt 16:24)

<u>Reflection:</u>

The Christian life does not promise happiness. It does not promise to be easy or carefree. It does, however, promise joy for all eternity, when we accept the challenges, pains, and trials, and walk humbly with Christ.

Let us pray: Lord, today, help me to die to myself. Help me to pick up my cross and walk humbly with your Son.

The Gift of Peace

Jeanne:

When Tom Junior, and then Tom Senior, and then Laurie died, I would go to the adoration chapel and concentrate on the Holy Eucharist. Every time, that peace beyond all understanding would come over me. That's a gift, and I'm very grateful for it.

Scripture:

Have no anxiety at all, but in everything, by prayer and petition, with thanksgiving, make your requests known to God. Then the peace of God that surpasses all understanding will guard your hearts and minds in Christ Jesus. (Phil 4:6-7)

Reflection:

What anxieties are you experiencing right now? Hand them over to God. Use a physical motion, forming a cradle with your hand and envisioning your troubles and worries held there. Then hold them up to God, offering a simple prayer such as this: Here, God. Here are all my problems, everything that's troubling me. I trust you to take care of it. Thank you.

Now, spend a moment basking in the peace of knowing that He will, indeed, take care of it.

The Repentant Sinner

Jeanne:

I am so very impressed when a person turns away from a sinful lifestyle and chooses God. The Bible tells us, "there is more joy in heaven over one sinner who repents than over ninety-nine righteous people who have no need of repentance." It must make our Lord so incredibly happy, when someone chooses Him!

Scripture:

"What man among you having a hundred sheep and losing one of them would not leave the ninety-nine in the desert and go after the lost one until he finds it? And when he does find it, he sets it on his shoulders with great joy and, upon his arrival home, he calls together his friends and neighbors and says to them, 'Rejoice with me because I have found my lost sheep.' I tell you, in just the same way there will be more joy in heaven over one sinner who repents than over ninety-nine righteous people who have no need of repentance." Luke 15:4-7

Reflection:

Christians are called to forgive one another, and we are also called to forgive ourselves.

Do you continue to harbor guilt for a sin that you have confessed with true repentance? Trust in Christ's mercy. Your sins are forgiven. Heaven rejoices!

Let us pray: Eternal God, in whom mercy is endless and the treasury of compassion inexhaustible, look kindly upon us, and increase your mercy in us, that in difficult moments, we might not despair nor become despondent, but with great confidence submit ourselves to your Holy Will, which is Love and Mercy itself.

(Prayer from the Chaplet of Divine Mercy)

Always There

Once you fall in love with Christ in the Holy Eucharist, your life will be changed forever. You will always look to Him for your joy, your peace, and your wisdom. It doesn't mean that life will always be easy, but you will know without a doubt that you don't have to walk the rough road alone. He is always there for you.

Scripture:

"And behold, I am with you always, until the end of the age." (Matt 28:20)

Reflection:

Spend a moment in silent prayer, aware of Christ's presence.

Let us pray: O Sacrament Most Holy, O Sacrament Divine, all praise and all thanksgiving be every moment thine. (Repeat three times)

Basking in God's Love

<u>Jeanne:</u>

I love to bask in God's love. When I would bring Patrick to the hospital for his hour of exercise, I would go down to the chapel to sit with the Holy Eucharist. After I had done all my praying, I would just sit in the quiet, gaze at the tabernacle, and bask in the love of the Lord.

<u>Scripture:</u>

The Lord, your God, is in your midst,
    a mighty savior,
Who will rejoice over you with gladness,
    and renew you in his love,
Who will sing joyfully because of you,
    as on festival days. (Zeph 3:17)

<u>Reflection:</u>

The scriptures are filled with examples of God's love for us. Psalm 139:2 tells us that He cares so deeply for us, He knows our most mundane movements. In Luke 12:7, Christ tells us that even the hairs on our head are counted! Moreover, He has such great love for us, He sent His only begotten son, that we might have eternal life (cf John 3:16).

When's the last time you basked in God's love? There's no time like the present!

Let us pray: Lord, help me to better understand your deep and abiding love for me. Help me to bask in your love!

A Commandment with a Promise

<u>Jeanne:</u>

These two old men – of course, I'm 88 and have no business calling anybody old – but these two old men hit me when I was driving. The first man hit me on the left side, and it was bad. While mine was in the shop, I had to get a rental car. I could hardly drive the thing. I didn't know which buttons to push, and I had to ask people in parking lots how to unlock the doors.

I was so happy when I finally got my car back! And then another old man hit me on the right side! After that, someone said to me, "Jeanne, you've got to tell these old men, if they want to hit on you, not to use a car!"

I got hit good, and was too sore to handle all the Christmas preparations. My children took care of it, though. They helped set up the Christmas tree, and Jack decorated the tree and the entire house. It looked fabulous. Jack did all the cooking, and Patrick carried down many of the gifts. They were wonderful.

<u>Scripture:</u>

Honor your father and your mother, as the Lord, your God, has commanded you, that you may have a long life and that you may prosper in the land the Lord your God is giving you. (Deut 5:16)

<u>Reflection:</u>

It's not always easy to honor our parents. We're busy, they're far away, they're difficult to deal with, they don't appreciate our efforts… maybe they weren't very good parents in the first place, and don't seem to deserve our honor! Yet, God's fourth commandment doesn't come with any "if's" – *if* you have time, *if* they live nearby, or *if* they have treated you well. Instead it comes with the reminder that God has, indeed, commanded us to do so. It also comes with a promise – that, by showing honor to your parents, you will enjoy a long life and prosperity.

Let us pray: Father, forgive me for the times I have failed to honor my parents. Heal the hurts they have afflicted on me, and the hurts I have inflicted upon them, and help me to treat them with honor from this moment forward.

Mary and the Church

Jeanne:

I once participated in an interdenominational Bible study where we would all go around the room and give our opinion about something. One day I said, "This isn't actually what we're talking about, but I feel called to talk about something that I feel is terribly tragic. One of the main things that separates Catholics from other Christians is that you all believe we worship the Blessed Lady. That is wrong. We are forbidden to worship her."

And then I said, "When you think about it, the fourth commandment is to honor your mother and father. If God was saying to us that you need to honor your father and your mother, what makes you think that He wouldn't demand that of Himself? That he would not want to honor His own mother?"

I received many letters and phone calls thanking me. They had always thought that we were *worshiping* the Blessed Mother. We do *honor* her, but we don't *worship* her. She was assumed into heaven, carried by the angels, but Jesus ascended, on His own power. The Blessed Mother can't work miracles. She can pray and convince her Son. The first miracle He worked, he did because she asked for it.

Scripture:

When the wine ran short, the mother of Jesus said to him, "They have no wine." [And] Jesus said to her, "Woman, how does your concern affect me? My hour has not yet come." His mother said to the servers, "Do whatever he tells you." Now there were six stone water jars there for Jewish ceremonial washings, each holding twenty to thirty gallons. Jesus told them, "Fill the jars with water." So they filled them to the brim. Then he told them, "Draw some out now and take it to the headwaiter." So they took it. And when the headwaiter tasted the water that had become wine, without knowing where it came from (although the servers who had drawn the water knew), the headwaiter called the bridegroom and said to him, "Everyone serves good wine first, and then when people have drunk freely, an inferior one; but you have kept the good wine until now." (John 2:3-10)

Reflection:

The Church teaches us that Christ's words from the cross, "Behold, your mother!" (John 19:27) were not intended solely for the disciple John, but for all of Christ's beloved disciples.

With one of his last breaths, Christ gave his Mother, Mary, to *you*, His beloved disciple. He didn't give her to you so that you might worship her. Worship is reserved for the Godhead, alone. Honor, reverence, and love, however, are required for every parent, including your Heavenly Mother.

How is your relationship with the Blessed Mother? How can you honor her today?

Let us pray: Hail Mary, full of grace, the Lord is with thee. Blessed art thou among women, and blessed is the fruit of thy womb, Jesus. Holy Mary, Mother of God, pray for us sinners, now and at the hour of our death. Amen.

Saying No

Jeanne:

Once all my children were grown, I began to serve on a number of different boards for various charities. At one point in time, I was serving on eight different boards.

And then we learned that my daughter Laurie was dying from cancer. I spent a day with her and she said, "Mother, I know how busy you are. I can't thank you enough for spending this time with me."

I thought, *The day I am too busy for any one of my children...* and I resigned from all eight of those boards. Spending time with my children, even though they were grown, was simply more important.

Scripture:

Who can find a woman of worth?
    Far beyond jewels is her value...
She is clothed with strength and dignity,
    and laughs at the days to come.
She opens her mouth in wisdom;
    kindly instruction is on her tongue.
She watches over the affairs of her household,
    and does not eat the bread of idleness.
Her children rise up and call her blessed;
    her husband, too, praises her:
"Many are the women of proven worth,
    but you have excelled them all."
Charm is deceptive and beauty fleeting;
    the woman who fears the Lord is to be praised.
                        (Prov 31:1, 25-30)

Reflection:

We live in a world filled with demands. Saying "no" can be an incredibly difficult thing, especially when we're saying "no" to an important cause. Sometimes, though, our "no" provides someone else with the opportunity to say "yes." Sometimes, our "no" allows us to say "yes" to something of even greater import.

Take a moment to consider the demands in your life. Are any of them discretionary? Might God be asking you to say "no," so that you can then say "yes" to something else?

Let us pray: Heavenly Father, reveal to me any activities that are not in keeping with your Holy Will. Help me to say "no" to the things you do not wish for me, and "yes" to those you do.

Missionary Discipleship

<u>Jeanne:</u>

There's a particular quote from Pope Francis that I love, so I printed off a stack and I keep them in my car. I never know when I might want to share it with someone. Just recently, I felt led to give it to a man who is particularly close to my heart.

He called me a few weeks later and said he wanted to go to lunch. When we did, he shared with me that the quote had touched him deeply. He's a grown man, but he cried several times. "I just want you to know that I have always gone to church," he told me, "but my lifestyle hasn't been what it should be. I want so badly to be close to God."

We sat there for two hours, and the whole conversation centered around his desire to be closer to God.

<u>Scripture:</u>

Andrew, the brother of Simon Peter, was one of the two who heard John and followed Jesus. He first found his own brother Simon and told him, "We have found the Messiah" (which is translated Anointed). Then he brought him to Jesus. Jesus looked at him and said, "You are Simon the son of John; you will be called Cephas" (which is translated Peter). (John 1:40-42)

<u>Reflection:</u>

We may never know how the small things we do to share the faith with others will impact them. Andrew told his brother Simon Peter about Jesus, and Peter went on to become the first Pope. Jeanne shared a simple quote, and it started a man on a journey closer to God.

Are you ready to share the faith when the opportunity arises? How can you become better prepared?

Let us pray: Today, Lord, I resolve to take a single step towards better missionary discipleship. Please show me the way.

The Forgiving Father

Jeanne:

Here's the quote I shared with that man. It's from Pope Francis's book, *The Joy of Discipleship*:

> He is waiting for you,
>
> He is close to you,
>
> He loves you,
>
> He is merciful,
>
> He forgives you,
>
> He gives you the strength
>
> to begin again from scratch!

Scripture:

"So he got up and went back to his father. While he was still a long way off, his father caught sight of him, and was filled with compassion. He ran to his son, embraced him and kissed him. His son said to him, 'Father, I have sinned against heaven and against you; I no longer deserve to be called your son.' But his father ordered his servants, 'Quickly bring the finest robe and put it on him; put a ring on his finger and sandals on his feet. Take the fattened calf and slaughter it. Then let us celebrate with a feast, because this son of mine was dead, and has come to life again; he was lost, and has been found.'" (Luke 15:20-24)

Reflection:

Meditate on these words from Pope Francis, taking them into your heart and accepting their truth.

Let us pray: Thank you, Lord, for waiting for me. Thank you for staying close to me. Thank you for loving me. Thank you for your mercy. Please forgive my many shortcomings, and give me the strength to do better with every moment of every day.

Greatest of These

Jeanne:

Patrick and I were walking with a doctor friend and his wife in the hospital one day. When we passed the information desk, the woman there smiled and said hello to us.

"Jeanne, everyone in this hospital has been trying to get that woman to say hello and smile for years, and no one has ever succeeded," our friend said. "How did you get her to do that?"

"One day I needed to ask her a question," I explained. "She didn't smile, but I said, 'Oh, you have a wonderful smile!' – I probably should go to confession. Regardless, when Christmas came shortly after that, I had Patrick give her a chocolate Santa Claus.

"You just can't give up on people," I added.

Scripture:

So faith, hope, love remain, these three; but the greatest of these is love. (1 Col 13:13)

Reflection:

Jeanne joked that she should go to confession for the white lie of telling the seemingly joyless woman that she had a wonderful smile, but was it really a lie? Every smile is beautiful, especially when it's brought about through love and kindness. We don't have to see a person's smile to appreciate this fact!

Jeanne's simple act of complementing the woman, and Patrick's equally simple act of giving her a token gift, seem to have wrought a change within her, while being equally rewarding to both Jeanne and Patrick.

What simple act of kindness can you perform today?

Let us pray: Dear Lord, help me to make somebody's day better today.

The Armor of God

Jeanne:

I keep my prayer life in a bag. There are prayers I've collected over the years – prayer cards from funerals and meditations from various saints. Some of these things have appeared suddenly in my bag, and I'll never know where they came from.

I take my prayer bag with me nearly everywhere I go, and I go through the prayers every day, praying each prayer, praying for the repose of every soul whose card is in there, reading through each reflection.

I pray the Divine Office as part of my prayers as a lay Franciscan, and I've read the Bible several times. I keep a regular holy hour of adoration. And, of course, I go to Mass every day.

Scripture:

Therefore, put on the armor of God, that you may be able to resist on the evil day and, having done everything, to hold your ground. So stand fast with your loins girded in truth, clothed with righteousness as a breastplate, and your feet shod in readiness for the gospel of peace. In all circumstances, hold faith as a shield, to quench all [the] flaming arrows of the evil one. And take the helmet of salvation and the sword of the Spirit, which is the word of God. With all prayer and supplication, pray at every opportunity in the Spirit. (Eph 6:13-18)

Reflection:

It is through our lives of prayer, through meditating on the scriptures, and receiving of the sacraments, that we put on our Christian armor.

Are you fully battle-ready? What practice can you take on that will make you better prepared?

Let us pray: Armor me, Lord, that I may resist evil and stand firm in faith.

PRAYER TO YOUR GUARDIAN ANGEL

Angel of God,
   my guardian dear,
To whom His love
   commits me here;
Ever this day(Or night)
   be at my side,
To light and guard,
   to rule and guide.

Amen.

GAN #076

20414

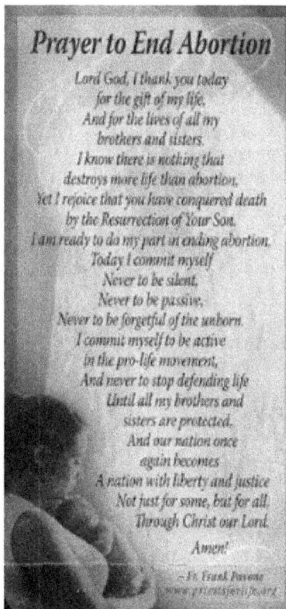

Prayer to End Abortion

Lord God, I thank you today
for the gift of my life,
And for the lives of all my
brothers and sisters.
I know there is nothing that
destroys more life than abortion,
Yet I rejoice that you have conquered death
by the Resurrection of Your Son.
I am ready to do my part in ending abortion.
Today I commit myself
Never to be silent,
Never to be passive,
Never to be forgetful of the unborn.
I commit myself to be active
in the pro-life movement,
And never to stop defending life
Until all my brothers and
sisters are protected,
And our nation once
again becomes
A nation with liberty and justice
Not just for some, but for all.
Through Christ our Lord.
Amen!

~ Fr. Frank Pavone
www.priestsforlife.org

Items from Jeanne's prayer bag. She is especially
devoted to the Prayer to End Abortion

75

Prayer of St. Pio of Pietrelcina

Stay with me, Lord, for it is necessary to have You present so that I do not forget You. You know how easily I abandon You.

Stay with me, Lord, because I am weak and I need Your strength, that I may not fall so often.

Stay with me, Lord, for You are my life, and without You, I am without meaning and hope.

Stay with me, Lord, for You are my light, and without You, I am in darkness.

Stay with me, Lord, to show me Your will.

Stay with me, Lord, so that I can hear Your voice and follow You.

Stay with me, Lord, for I desire to love You ever more, and to be always in Your company.

Stay with me, Lord, if You wish me to be always faithful to You.

Stay with me, Lord, for as poor as my soul is, I wish it to be a place of consolation for You, a dwelling of Your love.

Stay with me, Jesus, for it is getting late; the days are coming to a close and life is passing. Death, judgement and eternity are drawing near. It is necessary to renew my strength, so that I will not stop along the way, and for that I need You. It is getting late and death approaches. I fear the darkness, the temptations, the dryness, the cross, the sorrows. O how I need You, my Jesus, in this night of exile!

Stay with me, Jesus, because in the darkness of this life, with all its dangers, I need You.

Help me to recognize You as Your disciples did at the Breaking of the Bread, so that the Eucharistic Communion be the light which disperses the darkness, the power which sustains me, the unique joy of my heart.

Stay with me, Lord, because at the hour of my death I want to be one with You, and if not by Communion, at least by Your grace and love.

Stay with me, Jesus. I do not ask for divine consolations because I do not deserve them, but I only ask for the gift of Your Presence. Oh yes! I ask this of You!

Stay with me, Lord, for I seek You alone, Your Love, Your Grace, Your Will, Your Heart, Your Spirit, because I love You and I ask for no other reward but to love You more and more, with a strong and active love.

Grant that I may love You with all my heart while on earth, so that I can continue to love You perfectly throughout all eternity, dear Jesus. Amen!

For additional copies contact:

CAPUCHIN FRANCISCAN FRIARS
P.O. Box 839 ♦ Union City, NJ 07087
www.capuchinfriars.org
(201) 863-4036

"Stay with me Lord"
Prayer of
ST. PIO OF PIETRELCINA
after Communion

Acknowledgements

Jeanne:

I would first like to acknowledge the two men who encouraged me to write my story, and the countless others who have done the same since, especially Carol Gaal, who graciously began the process of writing down my stories.

Thank you, as well, to those many people who have prayed for me and my family over the years. Your kindness and support mean a great deal to me. While I can't possibly list everyone who has been a blessing to me, I'd like to especially thank Dr. John and Theresa Schutzman, Mike and Kathy Hirsch, Bob and Deborah Roberts, and Marty and Lorita Doucette. Finally, I'd like to thank my dear friends Christine Hackl and Mary Jane Baxter for their many kindnesses to my family.

When so many people suggested I write my story, I looked up to heaven and said, "God, if You want me to write a book, you will have to find me the time." He did one better. He found me the person. Thank you, God, for answering that prayer – and so many others.

Stephanie:

Endless gratitude goes out to Our Heavenly Father for blessing me with a job I love, and for the opportunity to collaborate on this book. Thank you to Jeanne for her example of strength and faith, and for allowing me to chronicle her story. Thank you to Beth Leonard, who not only introduced me to Jeanne, but also gave me a sneak peek at her book, *Praying Your Child Through Anything.* Beth's chapter about Jeanne provided much-appreciated insights for the "Child-Proof" story.

Finally, many thanks to Our Blessed Mother, who constantly intercedes for me and mine.

J + M + J

Notes:

[1] The full text of Jeanne's father's letter to his family:

I would like to acknowledge and thank my loving wife, Leona, for all she has done for me over these many years. I want her to know of my appreciation for her undying efforts to make my life easier, for her support in my efforts to make a reasonably good living for our family, and for her help and assistance in a spiritual and religious way. I have been singularly blessed in this regard. I beg her forgiveness for my many shortcomings.

To all of the children, I wish to say thanks for living upright and exemplary lives and for making it possible for us to be proud of you.

I take this opportunity to express my thanks to God for giving me the faith, a wonderful wife, and a fine family of whom I am justly proud, along with sufficient wealth for freedom from want. He sure has been extraordinarily generous to me.

For the future, I remind you that only one thing is necessary, and that is to save your immortal soul. So love one another and help one another, especially if they are in need. Keep the faith, the commandments. May God's choicest blessings be yours and may we meet in eternity. Your loving husband and father.

[2] https://www.catholicnewsagency.com/column/the-bride-and-the-bridegroom-at-the-supper-of-the-lamb-1867

About the Co-Author

Stephanie Engelman is a personal historian who enjoys chronicling the lives of others and learns from every story she writes. Stephanie is also a professional public speaker and the author of *A Single Bead*, an award-winning novel about the power of the Rosary. Her latest book, *Bead by Bead: The Sorrowful Mysteries for Children*, is designed to help children learn to meditate upon the Passion narrative as they pray the Rosary. In her free time, Stephanie enjoys spending time with her husband and five children, taking long walks with the dog, and any excuse to get outside to enjoy God's beautiful creation.

You can learn more about Stephanie by visiting her website, www.StephanieEngelman.com.

To learn more about having a personal history written for yourself or a loved one, please email Stephanie at Stephanie@inkwellwrites.com or visit her company's website, www.iwpersonalhistories.com.

Also by Stephanie Engelman

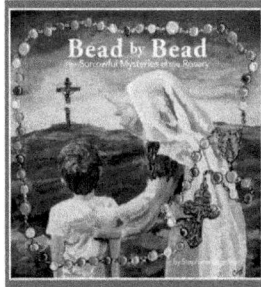

Contact Stephanie to learn about this
& other speaking topics: